Lost Kitten

Di Taylor

T0347346

Name _____

Age _____

Class _____

UNIVERSITY PRESS

OXFORD

UNIVERSITY PRESS

Great Clarendon Street, Oxford OX2 6DP

Oxford University Press is a department of the University of Oxford.
It furthers the University's objective of excellence in research, scholarship,
and education by publishing worldwide in

Oxford New York

Auckland Cape Town Dar es Salaam Hong Kong Karachi
Kuala Lumpur Madrid Melbourne Mexico City Nairobi
New Delhi Shanghai Taipei Toronto

With offices in

Argentina Austria Brazil Chile Czech Republic France Greece
Guatemala Hungary Italy Japan South Korea Poland Portugal
Singapore Switzerland Thailand Turkey Ukraine Vietnam

OXFORD and OXFORD ENGLISH are registered trade marks of
Oxford University Press in the UK and in certain other countries

ISBN: 978 0 19 440086 2

Printed in China

Illustrations by: Genny Haines
With thanks to Sally Spray for her contribution to this series

Reading Dolphins
Notes for teachers & parents

📖 Using the book

1 Begin by looking at the first story page (page 2). Look at the picture and ask questions about it. Then read the story text under the picture with your students. Use section 1 of the CD for this if possible.

2 Teach and check the understanding of any new vocabulary. Note that some of the words are in the **Picture Dictionary** at the back of the book.

3 Now look at the activities on the right-hand page. Show the example to the students and instruct them to complete the activities. This may be done individually, in pairs, or as a class.

4 Do the same for the remaining pages of the book.

5 Retell the whole story more quickly, reinforcing the new vocabulary. Sections 2 and 3 of the CD can help with this.

6 If possible, listen to the expanded story (section 4 of the CD). The students should follow in their books.

7 When the book is finished, use the **Picture Dictionary** to check that students understand and remember new vocabulary. Section 5 of the CD can help with this.

💿 Using the CD

The CD contains five sections.

1 The story told slowly, with pauses. Use this during the first reading. It may also be used for "Listen and repeat" activities at any point.

2 The story told at normal speed. This should be used once the students have read the book for the first time.

3 The story chanted. Students may want to chant along with the story.

4 The expanded story. The story is told in a longer version. This will help the students understand English when it is spoken faster, as they will now know the story and the vocabulary.

5 Vocabulary. Each word in the **Picture Dictionary** is spoken and then used in a simple sentence.

Toby the kitten wakes up.

Oh, no. Where am I?

Trace and write.

kitten kitten

sun

tree

leg

nest

3

Toby sees a bird.

I am lost.
Can you help me?

Circle yes or no.

1. Toby lives in a tree.

   yes

   (no)

2. The bird lives in a tree.

   yes

   no

3. There are five baby birds.

   yes

   no

4. The bird has a nest.

   yes

   no

5. Toby has a nest.

   yes

   no

6. The bird is blue.

   yes

   no

7. Toby is red.

   yes

   no

I am sorry.
I can't help you.
I live here in this nest.

Circle.

❶ The bird lives in a (**nest**) / **house** .

❷ **The bird** / **Toby** is lost.

❸ The bird **can** / **can't** help.

❹ Toby lives in a **nest** / **house** .

❺ The nest is in a **tree** / **house** .

❻ Toby is black and **red** / **white** .

Toby sees a spider.

Can you help me?
I am lost.

Number.

flower [3]   Toby [ ]

grass [ ]   spider [ ]

web [ ]   tree [ ]

I live here in this web.
I am sorry.
I can't help you.

Circle yes or no .

1. Toby is at home.

   yes

   ~~no~~ *(circled)*

2. The spider is in
   a web.

   yes

   no

3. The spider can
   help Toby.

   yes

   no

4. Toby is in a web.

   yes

   no

5. The spider has
   four babies.

   yes

   no

6. The spider is brown.

   yes

   no

7. Toby is in a tree.

   yes

   no

I am lost.
Can you help me?
This is your house.

Trace and write.

house house

bat

cat

tree

door

Hi, Mommy!
This is my house.
I am home!

Trace and tell the story.

1. Toby is a kitten _____ .

2. The kitten is lost _____ .

3. He sees a bird _____ .

4. He sees a spider _____ .

5. He sees a house _____ .

6. Toby is at home _____ .

Picture Dictionary

bat   cat

bird   door

blue   flower

brown   grass

house spider

kitten sun

leg tree

nest web

red white

Dolphin Readers

Dolphin Readers are available at five levels, from Starter to 4.

The Dolphins series covers four major themes:

Grammar, Living Together, The World Around Us, Science and Nature.

For each theme, there are two titles at every level.

Activity Books are available for all Dolphins.

All Dolphins are available on audio CD.
(2 TITLES ON EACH CD ◎ SEE TABLE BELOW)

Teacher's Notes are available at **www.oup.com/elt/dolphins**

	Grammar	Living Together	The World Around Us	Science and Nature
Starter	• Silly Squirrel • Monkeying Around	• My Family • A Day with Baby	• Doctor, Doctor • Moving House	• A Game of Shapes • Baby Animals
Level 1	• Meet Molly • Where Is It?	• Little Helpers • Jack the Hero	• On Safari • Lost Kitten	• Number Magic • How's the Weather?
Level 2	• Double Trouble • Super Sam	• Candy for Breakfast • Lost!	• A Visit to the City • Matt's Mistake	• Numbers, Numbers Everywhere • Circles and Squares
Level 3	• Students in Space • What Did You Do Yesterday?	• New Girl in School • Uncle Jerry's Great Idea	• Just Like Mine • Wonderful Wild Animals	• Things That Fly • Let's Go to the Rainforest
Level 4	• The Tough Task • Yesterday, Today and Tomorrow	• We Won the Cup • Up and Down	• Where People Live • City Girl, Country Boy	• In the Ocean • Go, Gorillas, Go